Presented to

Daniel Brennan

from

Mommy + Daddy

on

Easter, 1981

I Speak to God
Prayers for Children

by
Sister Margaret Bradley

Illustrated by
Diane Matthes

Regina Press
New York

First published in Great Britain in 1979 by
KEVIN MAYHEW LTD.

© Copyright 1979 by Kevin Mayhew Ltd

ISBN 0 905725 64 6

Nihil obstat   R.J.Cuming, D.D. Censor
Imprimatur   David Norris, V.G.
Westminster, 14th February, 1979

A Message from the Cardinal

My dear children,
I am glad to have this chance of
writing just to you and about this book.
It has been written specially for you and
I hope you will use it every day
to help you to pray. This is why
I am writing this note at the beginning
— to encourage you to go on praying.

God our Father is so good to us
all. It is only right that we should
praise and thank him for his kindness to
us. When we praise and thank him, we
pray. And God our Father wants us to
pray to him.

The prayers in this book will help you
to turn everything into prayer. Do try to
pray every day. That would be wonderful.
God our Father loves each one of you
and he will always be with you to help
you. And please, sometimes pray for me.

May God bless you all.

✠ Cardinal Basil Hume
Archbishop of Westminster

About Praying

Do you really want to pray?
That's great!
That's the first step.
Now, when you really
want something badly
you ask for it, don't you?
So, why not ask God our Father
to help you pray?
Just simply, like this —

> God, my loving Father,
> I want to talk to you;
> I want to pray.
> Please help me to pray well.

There you are!
That's an 'asking' prayer.
You're talking to God, our Father,
and he's really listening.
He will help you.

But he wants us to help ourselves too.
So, if we want to pray well,
we must open up our eyes,
our ears and our hearts.

God is speaking to us
through our beautiful world;
through the things that happen there,
and through the people
who live and work there.

We must try to
    Look well,
    Listen carefully,
    and then,
    Pray.

We have so much to tell God
about our world.
It's beauty and it's greatness
lie open before us.
The trees, the fields, the birds,
the sun, the sky, the running water;
every living creature that crawls
or climbs or swims,
speaks to us of our Father — God.
When we hear, and watch and wonder,
we've just got to praise and thank him.

    How do you do it, God?
    The world you have given us is beautiful.
    I love it.
    I'm glad I'm here to enjoy it.
    Thank you, God.

Praying would be so much easier
if only we could remember
that God is with us,
and that, through our Baptism,
we are his children.
As children of God, then,
there will be so many things
that we'll want to share with Him.
We'll want to talk with his Son, Jesus,
who is our brother.
There will be times, too, when we'll
want to talk with Mary our heavenly Mother,
and the Saints.
We'll want to share our joys and troubles
with them; speak to them about our fears,
our hopes, our dreams.
We'll want to talk to them about ourselves,
our families and our friends. We'll want
to remind them about the sick, those who
can't find work, the poor, the lonely, old
people and ever such a lot of other things.

Jesus has shown us how to pray.
Jesus prayed often.
He prayed alone;
when he was with the crowds;
when he was with his friends.

He prayed in the boat on the water;
on the mountain side;
in people's homes.
He prayed for the sick,
the poor,
the rich,
and all those who were sad
or in any sort of trouble.
He prayed for all of us.

Standing, sitting, kneeling, lying down,
always he was very sure that his Father
was near. And so he'd turn to him and
ask for the help and strength he needed,
for himself and others.

And he told us —
   'Rise up and pray' *(Luke 2:22)*
   'You don't have to stand out in
   the streets when you pray' *(Matthew 6:7)*
   'You don't have to use lots of
   words' *(Matthew 6:7)*

We can turn to God our Father, in our
secret heart and talk to him about what
we see, and hear, and touch and feel.
The radio, television, the newspapers,

our friends, the busy streets, the world
about us and the weather will provide us
with millions of chances to pray.

We need to pray.
    Jesus, our brother and friend,
    thank you for teaching us how to pray.
    We need to thank you for all your kindness.
    We need to praise you always.
    We need your help so much every day,
    We need to be forgiven.
    We want to pray.
    Please help us, Amen.

You're praying now.
Keep going!
And I shall pray with you.

Sister Margaret

9

I belong

God, I belong to you.
I want to do the things
    that please you.

In the name of the Father,
and of the Son,
and of the Holy Spirit.
Amen.

A morning prayer

Good morning, God, it's me.
Thank you for looking after
    me last night.
I slept very well
and the bed was cosy.
It's a beautiful morning
and I'm so glad to be alive.
Thank you, God, thank you.

My morning offering

Dear God, I offer you this day
and all my work and prayer and play.
Keep me in your loving care.
Teach me always how to share.

My Dad

You must know my Dad, God.
There's no one else quite like him.
That's what I think.
He's so strong, and he works so hard.
Sometimes we play games in the park,
and sometimes he takes us to the sea-side.
It's great fun!
Please keep him good and strong and happy.

My Mom

My Mom is always busy, God.
She shops and cooks and cleans and sews,
and chats to people that she knows.
I love her, God, she's good to us,
and I think my favorite day
in all the year is Mother's Day.
Please God, help my Mom!

My Brother

Lord, you know my brother.
He laughs and cries and kicks and screams,
plays with toys, and sometimes dreams.
He picks up this and puts down that,
looks at the patterns on the mat.
All day long he'll never stop
— he's going like a spinning top.
He's my brother, he's only two
— Lord, for him, I'm thanking you.

Prayer for a Sick Friend

Remember my friend, God.
You know all about him, anyway.
He's off from school these days
    with chicken-pox.
It's been two weeks now
and I miss him.
I wish I was off too;
school is not so good without him.
Hurry up and get him better — please!

Me

Lord, you love me.
Thank you for loving me.
Sometimes I'm good and helpful,
sometimes I'm selfish.
But you go on loving me all the time.

Lord, accept me as I am;
I try to do the best I can.
I'm no angel, as you see;
I need your help to strengthen me.

Friends

They are very special to me, Lord,
and I love them.
Thank you for giving me friends, Lord.
I share my time with them.
I love to chat with them.
We laugh together.
I trust them, and I know
that they trust me.
It's great to have friends, Lord.
Bless all my friends — please.

My Home

I'm glad I have a home, Lord,
but there are many children
who are not so lucky.
Some are homeless because
they have no parents,
others because of war,
or floods or earthquakes.
Please, Lord, help all those
children and all people who
are not as fortunate as I am.

A Rainy Day

It tumbles in thick, white sheets
from the dark sky.
Splish! splash! splish! splash!
It bounces off the road
and runs along the gutter.
I love the gurgling sound it makes.
It's great to watch it dance
on every surface.
And as I stare I wonder,
and thank you, God,
for the life rain gives to man,
and beast and flower.

A Windy Day

I couldn't catch it!
My hat blew off
and rolled along the pavement.
I ran after it.
And just as I stooped to pick it up,
it was off again!
I was blown along too.
So were the leaves and everything.
What a wind!
So powerful and strong.
God, I thought of you.

Brown Paper

Brown paper makes me think of you, God
Crushed and crumpled there it lies,
in the wind it flutters by,
dashing here, and dashing there —
Lord, I stop and stand and stare.
Now at last it's reached the gutter,
Soon it's off with sudden splutter.
Wrapped around a nearby tree
where it's plain for all to see.
But at last it drops from that,
worn and torn, like a battered hat.

Fog

Lord, what is it?
Like a great, gray sheet
it falls from the sky;
smothers all that passes by.
It feels so damp and smells so foul;
makes me cough, and my dog howl.
Just look at the traffic as it goes —
    so slowly.
    It's crawling.
    Where?
    Who knows.
Lord, look after the travellers as they go.

A Blue Sky

It's only blue sometimes,
But when it is, God, it's beautiful.
You are wonderful, great and mighty God.
Like the sky, your love
never seems
to end.

The Snail

You protect the snail, Lord.
You've made him wonderfully.
   with head twisting this way and that,
   his body all chubby and fat.
   Two horns beat the air,
   as I stand there and stare,
at the beautiful shell on his back.

Looking at a Worm

Pink and long with circles fine,
I watch you crawl without a spine.
You push and pull and press along,
with a slither, a slip and a slide.
Then slowly, towards a clump of leaves,
you drag your body and easily hide.
   It's interesting to watch, Lord.
   Even the worm is so perfect;
   so clever; so beautiful.
Thank you for taking care of him too.

Flowers

A bunch of flowers!
Wow, that's gorgeous!
Where's the smell coming from?
Ah, there it is!
They're beautiful —
rust, yellow and white —
chrysanthemums
Have you made them God,
long stem and all?
How wonderful!

Springtime

What a wonderful time it is, Lord.
I watch, and look, and listen —
   birds build, lambs play,
   flowers grow,
   farmers sow
   seeds for a new day.
It's just great to be alive
in Springtime, Lord.
We praise and bless you, Lord.

Summer

Holidays have come at last,
and the long hot days of
   summer are here.
I love this time of year, Lord,
and I thank you for
   the joy it brings
to the tired;
the old
and children.

Autumn

Short days,
long nights,
ripe berries,
golden fruits,
animals hoarding,
farmers storing,
leaves tumbling all the time,
what further need of sign?
It's autumn, Lord.
You send each season in turn.
Thank you for the beauty
and splendour of each.

Winter

Lord, it's icy cold and snow is falling,
it's white and thick and powdery.
Like a great blanket it spreads
itself quietly over the earth.
There's hush and stillness everywhere.
Till a blackbird calls from a nearby wall,
I hardly know I'm alive at all.
What was it like when you were small?

A Sad Child

You care about me, Lord.
You really know how I feel inside.
But other people — they don't seem to care
and I can't tell them.
    I can't put it all into words, Lord.
    But you know what I'm thinking, Lord.
    You really know and you care.
    I love you Lord.
    Thank you for caring.

Our Cat

He's a beautiful pet, God.
Look at his lovely black coat
    — so shiny and sleek.
He moves along so quietly
    on those four velvet paws.
I know when he's angry,
    or in good form.
All the things he can do . . .
    help me to think about you.
Thank you, God, for our cat,
    and for all pets.

Television

You know how much
   I love to watch it, Lord.
I can't pull myself away
   when bed-time comes.
I learn so much,
   and it's so much fun.
Lord, thank you for all the wonderful
   gifts you have given
   to actors
   and singers
   and musicians.
Help them Lord
   to use your gifts well.
Thanks for that funny story tonight, Lord.
   It was great.

Presents

That was a lovely present
I had from my friend, Lord.
I love reading books,
and this one looks exciting.
My friend is so good to me.
Thank you, Lord, for my friend.

More About Presents

God, our Father,
you have given us so many presents;
so many good things.
You have given us life . . .
    I can run and skip and jump.
    I can laugh and sing
      and read and write.
    I can think and learn
      and paint and sew.
There are so many things
    that I can do —
thank you for all
    these wonderful presents, God.
May I praise you always
    by using them well. Amen.

Wheels

You remember I was telling you
   about the bicycle, Lord.
Well, it's so much fun.
Mind you, I've fallen off it
   plenty of times and cut my knees,
but I still enjoy the feel
   of moving along so fast.

John hasn't got one.
I know I should share mine
   a bit more, but I'm selfish.
I let him stand and look on.
Please help me to share my toys, Lord.

A Packed Bus

'Come on! Move along!
Five standing inside only!
The rest upstairs, please!'
That's the conductor, Lord.
He must be worn out with all of us.
  Give him patience, Lord.
  And help the driver too.
  It's not an easy job to
    drive a bus in all this traffic.
  You *will* look after him, Lord,
    won't you?

Newspapers

One comes into our house every day, Lord.
I'm not very good at reading yet,
but I can read some of it.
I see some very sad pictures, too.
All these people are yours, Lord.
  Some are bad and wicked,
  some are sad and suffering,
  some are lonely and old.
Please Lord, please help them ...
all of them, Lord.

A Prayer of Faith

God, you are my loving Father,
I believe in your love for me.
I believe in your son, Jesus.
He died for love of me.
But he is now risen.
He is alive. He is with us.
I believe that Mary is his mother,
    and mine too, and I thank you
for helping me to believe, God.

My Dog

You take care of every creature, God —
you want me to take care of my dog.
He's like a fox in colour and cunning,
I love to stand and watch him running
after this rabbit or dangerous rat.
He doesn't care at all about that.
Please help me to be kind to all my pets.

The Ladybird

Hey! Look! A ladybird!
Isn't it beautiful?
It's a reddish brown colour
with black spots on it's back.
It's moving slowly along my arm now,
and as I watch it go,
I think of you, God.
You put such wonderful colour
    into your world.
It could have been so dull otherwise.
Other children are gathering
around now to have a look.
You're great, God.
Oh! Zoom, zoom — she's gone!

A Special Honor

I won a prize in school today —
for work well done.
It was a story book — my favorite, Lord.
Just three of us won a prize, Lord.
Must work hard again tomorrow!
Nearly forgot to thank you
for helping me, Lord.
You did say we can do nothing
   without you,
and it's true.
Stay with us always, and help us.

To a Sparrow

God, your Son, Jesus,
told us that you take care of us.
I thought of his words today
as I watched you provide food
for the sparrow. And I prayed:
Chirp, chirp, little sparrow,
    so feathery and brown,
what are you looking for
    there on the ground?
No need to worry,
    no need to care,
here comes an old lady
    who's ready to share.
Swish, swish, how she scatters
    the crumbs around,
there, just before you,
    little sparrow so brown.
So eat and have plenty,
    invite your friends too,
God finds a way to feed
    — even you.

Trees

There is nothing so splendid
   as the tall tree
on the other side
   of the road, Lord.
I watch it all the year round.
Now the leaves are changing colour.
They hang like gold
   from all its branches.
In the breeze (because they're dying),
they shiver and rustle
   and slowly drop off and fall.
But in Spring time,
   there will be new leaves —
fresh and sappy and green —
a beautiful picture, Lord,
and a sure shelter
   for the birds of the air.

Trust

There is no one so great as you, God.
No-one so powerful and wise.
You are kind, loving, forgiving and strong.
I trust in your love for me.
I really do.
I'm so glad I belong to you.

Love

Jesus, my brother and friend,
    I love you.
You have done
    so much to help me.
I want to love you more.
Help me to be kind
    to those around me.
This will be the best way
    of showing that I love you.

People

There they are, Lord,
crowds of them in the street.
They're tall and short,
they're fat and slim.
Some are clever,
some are dim.
I wonder what they think of me
as I go by and look and see
their beauty or their ugliness.
I wonder do they think at all.
Have they got time for one so small?
God, please bless them all.

For the Lonely

So often in your life
    you were lonely, Lord.
To-day, our world is full
    of lonely people — young and old.
Please, Lord, think of them
    and help them.

For the Poor

I see them in the streets, Lord, ·
and they look so miserable.
You were once poor.
You know what I mean.
Please help the poor
to find happiness, food,
    clothes and shelter.

For Old People

Do not leave them alone
now that they are old and gray, Lord.
Keep watching over them
as they move slowly along towards you.
Make people kind towards them, Lord.
Thank you for the lives they have lived —
and will you help them
    to understand us, Lord?
It must be hard for them.

Water

It's fun to splash
   in the water so deep
with wellington boots
   upon my feet.
To sail a small boat
   in a very small pond,
what else is a puddle?
   Why look beyond?
   And even as my boat sails, Lord,
   I think about how useful water is.
   We use so much of it every day —
   to drink, and cook,
     and wash, and play.
   Thank you, God, for water.

At the Sea

How I love to play in the soft
   yellow sand at the sea-shore, Lord.
I could stay forever building castles
   and sailing 'sweet-paper boats'
   in the moats!
O thank you, Lord, thank you
   for the pleasure and
   the wonders of the sea.

Advent

A time of waiting, and watching, and praying.
A time of hoping, and longing, and saying:
  Come, Lord!
  Come, quickly!
  Come into our hearts, and be King.
Mary, our heavenly Mother,
as we wait to celebrate
  the birthday of Jesus,
please help us to think
  of other people.
Help us to work harder at home,
in school and in the classroom.
We can hardly wait for Christmas to come.
You see, we always get more toys,
new clothes and nice things to eat.
It's a great time and so exciting.
Help us to remember
that it is also *a time of giving*. Amen.

Christmas

Welcome Jesus!
We're so glad you've come among us;
like one of us.

That's why we pray:
   Thank God you came,
     to save the lame,
     the hungry and depressed.
   Thank God you came
     to serve and not to be served.
   Thank God you came,
     not for fame, but just to do
   the best for me,
     and mine, and everyone.
   Thank God you came!

Lent

It's Ash Wednesday, Lord.
Lent is just beginning —
Six weeks till Easter!
I'm not going to be gloomy during Lent.
You want us to be happy
    and cheerful.
I shall try really hard
    to help other people
    at this time.
I am your follower.
I want to be a good one.
Sometimes it's hard to follow you.
So please help me now. Amen.

Easter

Dead you were, and three days gone,
your friends began to sigh:
    What shall we do? We are so few.
    Indeed, we all may die.
As they began to ponder,
    their minds began to wander,
and a voice broke in the skies:
    He's risen! Risen! Risen!
    I've seen him with these eyes.
Some stood aghast, some ran so fast,
to find out for themselves:
    Indeed, the Lord is risen!
    No doubt!
    Shout out!
    Hurray!
    Alleluia!

Prayer to the Holy Spirit

Jesus, when you had gone back
to your Father,
the Apostles were lonely
and afraid.
They hid away in a big room,
and there, with Mary,
our heavenly mother,
they prayed
and waited for your help.
On Pentecost Sunday,
you sent your Holy Spirit on them.
That was a great day.
Your Spirit gave them courage
and strength
to speak out the truth about you —
about your life, death,
and resurrection.
They were so brave when
your Holy Spirit helped them.
Please send your Spirit
on us, Jesus.
May we always have the courage
to be honest
and do what is right. Amen.

Holy Communion

Jesus, you give people
yourself in Holy Communion.
I watch people go to receive you
from the priest on Sundays,
when I go to Mass.
I would like you to come to me.
Please help me to get ready
for this great gift of yourself.
You couldn't have given us any better gift.
You are the very best gift of all.
Praise and thanks to you, Jesus.
You give us yourself in Holy Communion.

For Our Parish and Priests

God, please bless our parish
and all our priests.
Ours is such a big parish,
and there is so much to be done.
Help us to think more of each other,
and to help where we can.

For Our School

Lord,
we come here every day to work.
Help us to work well.
Make our school a happy place
where we can enjoy ourselves,
as we learn about ourselves
and others.

For Leaders

You were a leader, Jesus,
you showed us how we should live
and love.
Help the leaders
of every country and group today.
May they follow your example
and be good leaders,
bringing joy, happiness and peace
to everyone. Amen.

In Time of Trouble

That's true, I'm in trouble again, Lord.
I don't know why! It just happens!
I don't want to be bad —
I don't really want to make others mad
But that's what happened again, Lord.
Do help me to try harder — please.

Sorrow

God, my loving Father,
because you are so good,
I am very sorry
for all the wrong things
I have done;
and with your help,
I shall try to do better.
Please help me. Amen.

At Night

It's night time, Lord,
and I'm getting ready for bed.
What a day . . .
the work, the trouble, the fun!
The good things, Lord,
the bad ones too —
they're gone,
they're over and done.
So I pray:
    Thank you, God, for another day.
    Keep me safe tonight —
    watch over all your children everywhere.
    Bless my mommy and daddy,
    all my aunties and uncles.
    Bless my nanna and grandad,
    and all my family and friends.
    Watch over all those who are sick tonight,
    and help all those
    who are tempted to do what is wrong.
    You're great, God.
    I know you can do all this,
    and more.

A Prayer to Our Lady

As we get ready for Christmas,
we think of the angel Gabriel —
God's great messenger,
who asked you to be
   the Mother of Jesus.
He said:
   Hail Mary, full of grace,
      the Lord is with thee.
   Blessed art thou amongst women,
   and blessed is the fruit
      of thy womb — JESUS.

You said that you would be
   the Mother of JESUS.
You *are* the Mother of JESUS.
You are my mother too.
You are the Mother of all and so,
as children in God's great family,
we pray:
   Holy Mary, Mother of God,
   pray for us sinners, now,
   and at the hour of our death. Amen.

Hope

So many things seem wrong
in our world, Lord.
People are afraid of war and sickness.
I am afraid too.
Afraid of the dark,
afraid of people who look cross.
But I hope you will help us, Lord.
Stay with us always.
You are so strong — so full of courage.
I hope you will never leave us.

The Lord's Prayer

The apostles often watched you pray, Jesus.
They must have wondered
  what it was all about.
They wanted to pray, too.
They asked you to show them
  how to pray.
You taught them this great prayer.
It's your prayer.
The Lord's prayer.
We say your prayer
when we pray together at Mass:
    Our Father, who art in heaven,
    hallowed be thy name;
    thy kingdom come:
    thy will be done
      on earth as it is in heaven.
    Give us this day our daily bread;
    and forgive us our trespasses
    as we forgive those
      who trespass against us;
    and lead us not into temptation,
    but deliver us from evil. Amen.
God is our Father.
May he be praised forever.

To the Saints

You are God's special friends,
and I thank him for all of you.
You followed his way
    of love and kindness,
and it wasn't always easy.
But you trusted him to help you,
    and he did.
Now that you are with him in heaven,
please pray for us.
Ask him to help us every day.
You're lucky to be with him forever.
He's so kind and loving.

Going to Church

Sometimes I like to go to church
to pray with your family, God,
but sometimes I feel so small;
    I feel lost.
And I can't understand
what the priest is saying,
the words are too hard.
But you know that I have come to pray —
you want me to be there.
You see me there, even if I feel lost,
and you're glad I have come.

Thank You, Lord!

Thank you, Lord,
for ash and elm and poplar tall.
Thank you, Lord,
for bush and briar and plant so small.
Thank you, Lord,
for eyes to see them all.
Thank you, Lord.

Thank you, Lord,
for colours red and green.
Thank you, Lord,
for every running stream.
Thank you, Lord,
for eyes to see them all.
Thank you, Lord.

Thank you, Lord,
a thousand times
    I thank you,
for all the beauty
    you have shown to me,
in every thing
    that lives and breathes.
I praise and thank
    my saviour and my King.

Praying

It has been great
   to talk with you, Jesus
and with Our Father, God.
I thought it would be much harder,
but I know you have been helping me.
Thank you for your help.

We're so lucky to have Mary
   for our Mother.
She is praying for us.
Thank you, God,
   for our Mother Mary.

And thanks, too,
   for your great army of saints.
I am sure they pray for us, too.

May they go on praising you
   for ever and ever.
   I want to praise you, too.
   You are great, God, and I love you.
   May every star that shines,
   every bird that sings,
   every plant that grows
   praise and bless you forever. Amen.

64